SURVIVING CC
HEART FA

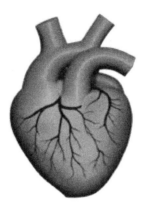

A Comprehensive Guide to Fluid-Induced Heart Failure

By

Dr. Bertha Arledge

COPYRIGHT PAGE

Table Of Contents

INTRODUCTION

My favorite aunt Martha was always in good health and active. She cherished spending time with her family, cooking, and gardening. Yet as she aged, she started to exhibit signs like exhaustion, breathlessness, and swelling in her legs.

She had a battery of testing, and congestive heart failure was identified (CHF). She was initially heartbroken by the information and concerned about how it would affect her life. But, she was able to control her condition and carry on leading a full life with the assistance of her medical team, me, and her family.

Martha's treatment program combined medication, dietary changes, and ongoing medical attention. She closely collaborated with her doctor to change the dosage of her medication, and because I was her favorite niece and had experience in this area, I was able to keep an eye on her symptoms. I also changed her diet, encouraging her to consume less salt and more fruits and vegetables.

My aunt Martha continued to participate in the activities she enjoyed despite being diagnosed with cancer. She kept working in the garden, pausing only when she needed to rest. She also discovered new exercises to keep herself in shape, like mild yoga and family walks.

Family was a significant support system for her as well. They assisted her with daily tasks as needed and pushed her to maintain her optimistic outlook and pay attention to her health. Her grandchildren frequently paid her visits, and she enjoyed watching them play.

Despite the challenges of having CHF, my aunt found comfort in her faith and the affection of her family. She was determined to continue enjoying life to the fullest and not let her illness define her. She was able to manage her disease and spend many more joyful years with her loved ones with the correct support and care. Please relax while I give you all the knowledge that has assisted my aunt and many others in managing this ailment and continuing to live their lives.

CHAPTER 1

Understanding Congestive Heart Failure (CHF)

- When the heart's capacity as a pump is insufficient to satisfy the body's demands, the condition is known as congestive heart failure (CHF).
- When the heart's capacity to pump blood is impaired due to several disease processes, it results in congestive heart failure.
- Congestive heart failure symptoms might range, but they may include the following:
  o Fatigue
  o decreased capacity for exercise
  o breathing difficulty
  o Swelling (edema) (edema)

A thorough physical examination, knowledge of the patient's medical history, and a few chosen laboratory tests are used to make the diagnosis of congestive heart failure.

- Congestive heart failure can be treated with lifestyle changes, addressing causes that may be changeable, drugs, heart transplants, and mechanical therapy.
- Congestive heart failure can develop in a variety of ways depending on the patient. In most cases, it might be serious.

A Life-Like Model of a Human Heart.

Congestive Heart Failure: What Is It?

The term "heart failure" refers to the heart's incapacity or failure to supply the nutrients and oxygen that the body's organs and tissues require. The fluid (mostly water) leaks from capillary blood vessels as a result of the decrease in cardiac output, the volume of blood that the heart pumps, which is insufficient to move the blood that is being pumped back to the heart from the body and lungs. This results in symptoms like edema, weakness, and shortness of breath.

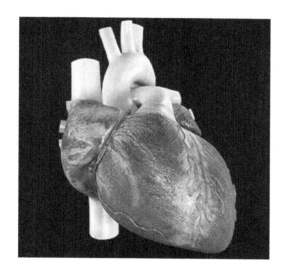

Understanding the Heart's and Body's Blood Flow

Blood is pumped from the right side of the heart to the lungs and from the left side to the rest of the body. By the vena cava, blood from the body reaches the right atrium. After that, it enters the right ventricle and is pumped to the lungs via the pulmonary artery, which transfers deoxygenated blood there. Red blood cells are filled with oxygen in the lungs, where it is then transported back to the left atrium of the heart by the pulmonary veins. The body's organs and tissues are then supplied with blood through the left ventricle. Red blood cells download oxygen into the organs, while carbon dioxide, a metabolic waste product, is added and expelled from the lungs. After that, blood flows back into the right atrium to restart the cycle. Because they transport oxygenated blood, the pulmonary veins are uncommon compared to the pulmonary artery. The roles of arteries and veins in the rest of the body are reversed in this situation.

When the left ventricle cannot pump blood to the body, fluid backs up and seeps into the lungs, resulting in left heart failure and shortness of breath. When the right ventricle is unable to efficiently pump blood to the lungs, right heart failure develops. The veins that carry blood to the heart may become backed up with blood and fluid. Fluid may seep into tissues and organs as a result of this.

Biventricular heart failure is the medical term for when both ventricles of the heart stop working properly at the same time. Since left heart failure is the most frequent cause of right heart failure, this frequently happens.

Picture of a cross-section of the heart.

Heart Cross Section

Aorta

Direction of blood flow

Pulmonary artery

Pulmonary veins

SA node

Left atrium

Right atrium

AV node

Vena cava

Right ventricle

Left ventricle

CHAPTER 2

What symptoms and indicators are present in congestive heart failure?

Breathing Difficulty

Shortness of breath is the hallmark and most prevalent symptom of left heart failure and may occur:

1. At rest;

2. By work or effort

3. While uncurled up (orthopnea)

4. When the person is awakened from sleep (paroxysmal nocturnal dyspnea); or

5. As a result of fluid (mostly water) buildup in the lungs or the heart's inability to function as efficiently as it could to pump blood to the body's organs under stress or effort.

Chest Ache

1. Chest pain or angina may be present, particularly if coronary heart disease is the underlying cause of the failure.

The left or right heart failure, or both

1. Individuals with right heart failure leak fluid into the organs and tissues that use the vena cava to transport blood to the right heart.

2. Water leaks into cell spaces as a result of backpressure in capillary blood vessels, and this fluid is frequently seen in the body's lowest regions.

3. Fluid builds up in the feet and ankles due to gravity, but as more fluid builds up, it may gradually spread to the lower legs as a whole.

4. Fluid can build up in the abdominal cavity and the liver, causing them to expand (hepatomegaly) (ascites).

5. The patient may have bloating, nausea, and abdominal pain with a sense of distension due to ascites and hepatomegaly.

6. Patients may exhibit signs of right heart failure, left heart failure, or both, depending on their underlying condition and the clinical context.

Congestive heart failure is most frequently brought on by coronary artery disease and excessive blood pressure (hypertension).

Angina or chest pain is a symptom of congestive heart failure.

What Are the Causes of Congestive Heart Failure?

The condition known as congestive heart failure occurs when the heart's capacity to pump blood is impaired by several disease processes. Namely in the USA. Congestive heart failure is most frequently brought on by:

- Cardiovascular disease
- Long-term alcohol consumption; hypertension, or high blood pressure
- Issues with the heart's valves
- Unknown (idiopathic) reasons, such as those that arise upon myocarditis recovery

Congestive heart failure can also result from

- thyroid issues
- irregular cardiac rhythms
- viral infections that cause the heart muscle to stiffen, and congestive heart failure.

Some drugs may cause the onset or worsening of lung disease in persons with congestive heart failure and underlying heart disease. Drugs may also result in sodium retention or have an impact on the strength of the heart muscle. Nonsteroidal anti-inflammatory drugs (NSAIDs), such as ibuprofen (Motrin and others), naproxen (Aleve and others), as well as some steroids, some type 2 diabetic treatments, such as rosiglitazone (Avandia) or pioglitazone (Actos), and some calcium channel blockers are examples of such pharmaceuticals (CCBs).

What Phases of Congestive Heart Failure are There?

A scale designed by the New York Heart Association is frequently used to assess the functional capabilities of heart failure.

The ability of the patient to function is frequently used to grade heart failure on a scale from I to IV.

1. Class 1: Patients in Class I are not restricted in their physical activity.

2. Class II: Individuals with a modest physical limitation who experience tiredness, palpitations, dyspnea, or angina

pain with a considerable increase in physical activity but who feel comfortable at rest.

3. Class III: Individuals who have a substantial restriction on physical activity and who experience weariness, palpitations, dyspnea, or angina pain with even routine activity but who are at ease at rest.

4. Class IV patients include those who are unable to engage in any physical activity without experiencing discomfort as well as those who exhibit heart failure or angina symptoms even when at rest; the patient's discomfort rises when engaging in any physical activity.

What are the Congestive Heart Failure Risk Factors?

As atherosclerotic heart disease frequently results in congestive heart failure, the risk factors are the same:

- poorly controlled high blood pressure
- high cholesterol
- diabetes
- smoking, and
- family history.

When the patient ages, heart valve dysfunction becomes a risk factor.

Heart failure can also be caused by other diseases, which come with their own set of risk factors and predispositions.

These factors may include

- systemic lupus erythematosus, sarcoidosis, amyloidosis,
- obstructive sleep apnea
- alcohol and drug addiction
- infections, and connective tissue disorders.

A change in their bodies can cause many individuals with stable congestive heart failure to decompensate. As an illustration, a patient with congestive heart failure might be doing well until they get pneumonia, a lung infection, or a heart attack.

The patient's heart may not have the capacity or reserve to meet the body's energy requirements and may not be able to respond to the body's changing environment.

If the patient consumes too much fluid, consumes too much salt, which can cause the body to retain water, or forgets to take their regular medicine, acute decompensation may result.

What Techniques and Exams are Used to Identify Congestive Heart Failure?

A medical emergency may arise from congestive heart failure, particularly if it acutely decompensates and the patient exhibits severe illness and inadequate breathing. The ABCs of resuscitation (Airway, Breathing, and Circulation) must be taken care of in this case, and congestive heart failure must also be identified.

The following are typical tests that are performed to aid in the diagnosis of congestive heart failure:

• An electrocardiogram (EKG, ECG) to measure the heart's rhythm, size of the ventricles, and blood flow to the heart muscle indirectly.

• A chest X-ray to check the size of the heart and whether or not the lungs are filled with fluid.

• Complete blood count (CBC), electrolytes, glucose, BUN, and creatinine are among the possible blood tests (to assess kidney function).

• B-type natriuretic peptide (BNP) testing can determine if a patient's shortness of breath is caused by congestive heart failure or by another condition. When these muscles are overworked, a substance that is stored in the heart ventricles may be released.

• To evaluate the anatomy and function of the heart, echocardiography or cardiac ultrasound testing is frequently advised. The test can also examine the blood flow within the heart, watch the heart chambers contract, and measure the ejection fraction (the percentage of blood expelled with each beat; normal range = 50% to 75%) in addition to assessing the heart valves and muscles.

Depending on the clinical scenario, several tests could be taken into consideration to assess and monitor a patient with suspected congestive heart failure.

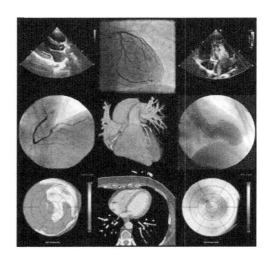

CHAPTER 3

Exactly How is Congestive Heart Failure Treated?

Congestive heart failure treatment aims to improve cardiac function so that it can supply the body with the necessary energy. Depending on the underlying cause of heart failure, specific treatments may include:

Therapies that reduce bodily fluids (diuretics)

The goal of treatment may be to reduce bodily fluid so that the heart does not have to work as hard to pump blood through the body's blood arteries. Limiting fluid intake and cutting back on salt consumption may be quite beneficial.

Typical Water Tablets or Diuretics Include:

- Hydrochlorothiazide
- bumetanide, and
- furosemide (Lasix)

Medicines

• ACE inhibitors (angiotensin-converting enzyme inhibitors) and ARBs (angiotensin receptor blockers) are medications that have also been shown to increase survival by lowering systemic resistance and favorably changing the hormonal environment, which affects cardiac performance; they are frequently used in combination with other medications.

Beta-blockers may drop blood pressure, increase cardiac output and ejection fraction, and positively respond to circulating epinephrine ("adrenalin").

• Digoxin (Lanoxin), an antiquated medication, might help boost cardiac output and manage symptoms.

- Spironolactone is a modern, very mild diuretic that has long-term advantages.

Modifying Cardiac Risk Factors

The mainstay of preventing congestive heart failure is the alteration of cardiac risk factors, which may also be advantageous for those who already have the condition.

Congestive heart failure treatment options include:

- Losing weight

- Workout
- quitting smoking
- Managing diabetes, high cholesterol, and blood pressure

A left ventricular assist device (LVAD), an implanted pump that helps the heart pump more blood, or even a heart transplant may be necessary for people with end-stage congestive heart failure (NYHA stage IV).

Congestive heart failure patients are not suitable for organ transplants; an LVAD may be a long-term solution.

How May Congestive Heart Failure Be Treated and Managed by Changes in Lifestyle?

- As soon as congestive heart failure is identified, therapy should begin.
- One of the most crucial components a patient can use to cure congestive heart failure is lifestyle adjustment.

Among these lifestyle modifications are those related to

- Diet
- Exercise
- Fluid balance, and
- Weight maintenance.

Salt, or sodium, causes the body to retain more fluid.

Nutrition and Exercise

Sodium

Sodium raises the amount of fluid that accumulates in human tissues. Patients become extremely sensitive to the amounts of salt and water they consume because their bodies are frequently clogged with extra fluid. Because fluid tends to build in the lungs and surrounding tissues, it is frequently advised to limit salt and fluid intake.

• Even with "no added salt," a daily sodium intake of 4 to 6 grams (4,000–6,000 mg) is still possible.

• It's generally recommended that people with congestive heart failure consume no more than 2 grams (2000 milligrams) of sodium each day.

• It's crucial to read food labels and keep track of your daily salt intake.

• Strict limitations on alcohol use.

Exercise

Congestive heart failure (CHF) management includes regular exercise since it can enhance heart health, lessen symptoms, and enhance the overall quality of life. It is crucial to remember that the type and intensity of exercise should be customized to the person's health status, symptoms, and degree of fitness. Here are some types of exercises a person with CHF can perform:

1. Aerobic exercise, which was long prohibited for those with congestive heart failure, helps people maintain their total functional ability, and quality of life, and may even extend their lives. Everybody's body has a different capacity to make up for a failing heart. When the cardiac muscles are weak to the same extent, people can exhibit a wide range of functional limitations. Regular exercise appears to offer considerable benefits when customized to the person's tolerance level and should only be employed when the person is compensated and stable.

2. Walking: Walking is a low-impact exercise that can help build muscles, lower blood pressure, and enhance

cardiovascular health. Start slowly and progressively pick up the pace and distance as you go.

3. Cycling is another low-impact workout that may be performed outside or on a stationary cycle. Leg strength and cardiovascular fitness can both be enhanced by it.

4. Swimming: Swimming is a low-impact workout that can increase muscular endurance and cardiovascular health. Also, it is gentle on the joints and might help lessen leg swelling.

5. Resistance training can assist increase muscle strength and endurance. Examples of resistance training include weightlifting and the use of resistance bands. This can lessen signs of weariness and enhance general fitness.

6. Yoga: Yoga is a low-impact workout that can assist increase strength, flexibility, and balance. Also, it can aid in lowering tension and anxiety, which is good for your general health and well-being.

NOTE

To create a safe and efficient exercise program for people with CHF, it's crucial to engage closely with a healthcare professional or trained exercise specialist. Based on the person's health and fitness level, they can assist in choosing the right degree of exercise intensity, duration, and frequency. To guarantee the best benefits and lower the risk of problems, regular monitoring and modifications to the fitness program may also be required.

Fluid Control

A patient's overall fluid intake needs to be controlled. Even though many persons with congestive heart failure use prescription diuretics to help with fluid excretion, an excessive intake of water and other fluids can interfere with the medication's ability to work. The adage "eight glasses of water a day is beneficial" most definitely does not apply to congestive heart failure sufferers. It is frequently recommended to patients with more severe forms of congestive heart failure to keep their daily fluid intake to no more than 2 quarts.

The aforementioned recommendations for fluid and sodium intake may change depending on how severe congestive heart failure is in a particular person, so they should be discussed with their doctor.

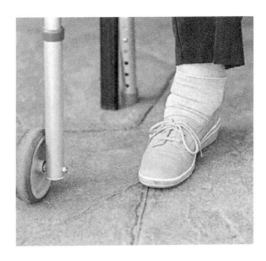

Diuretics can aid in the body's excess fluid removal.

Preserving Weight

• Regularly measuring the patient's body weight is a crucial tool for ensuring a proper fluid balance.

- An increase in body weight is a precursor to edema and can occur before symptoms like shortness of breath or swelling of the legs and other body parts are noticed.

• A doctor should be contacted if a patient experiences a weight gain of 2 to 3 pounds over 2 to 3 days. The doctor may then decide to increase the dosage of their diuretic or use other measures to stop the fluid buildup in its early stages before it worsens.

Diuretics can help in the elimination of excess fluid in the body.

CHAPTER 4

How Long Will Someone with Congestive Heart Failure Live?

The majority of the time, congestive heart failure is a progressive condition with periods of stability interspersed with sporadic clinical exacerbations. The way the disease develops in any one person, however, varies greatly. the variables that affect the prognosis (long-term outlook) for

Congestive heart failure includes:

- the kind of underlying heart disease
- the response to treatment
- the involvement of other organ systems and the severity of other comorbid illnesses
- the person's symptoms and level of impairment and other, less well-understood factors.

The prognosis for congestive heart failure is generally better than that found just ten years ago due to the availability of newer medications that may potentially favorably alter the course of the condition. It is not unusual to see a considerable spontaneous improvement in some circumstances, especially when the heart muscle dysfunction has just started to manifest. In some cases, this recovery can even be so great that heart function returns to normal.

Heart Failure Patients' Prognosis Is Highly Related to The Functional Class

The danger of abnormal cardiac rhythms is a significant issue in congestive heart failure (arrhythmias). Around 50% of deaths in people with congestive heart failure are caused by progressive heart failure. The significant other half is allegedly connected to severe arrhythmias.

The discovery that nonsurgical automatic implantable cardioverter/defibrillator (AICD) placement can significantly improve survival in people with severe congestive heart failure (defined by an ejection fraction below 30% to 35%) has been a significant advancement, and it has now become the standard of care in the majority of these patients.

A device known as a biventricular pacer can be used to correct a condition where the left and right sides of the heart don't beat in rhythm in some persons with severe heart failure and specific ECG abnormalities.

Can Congestive Heart Failure Be Avoided?

- Atherosclerotic heart disease is frequently the underlying condition that leads to congestive heart failure.
- Reducing those risk factors may aid in preventing congestive heart failure.
- They include quitting smoking and maintaining lifelong control of high blood pressure, high cholesterol, and diabetes.
- Alcohol and drug addiction may contribute to congestive heart failure
- high blood pressure and diabetes poses separate hazards for the condition.

Diastolic Dysfunction:

This type of CHF is characterized by stiffness of the heart muscle, which most frequently results from hypertension or age. The prognosis is excellent and the ejection fraction is normal. Shortness of breath results from a stiff heart muscle filling with blood at a higher pressure, which is conveyed to the lungs. The great long-term prognosis for patients with this illness must be underlined.

Quitting smoking can help prevent congestive heart failure.

How Can Congestive Heart Failure Be Managed?

Congestive heart failure sufferers can get help from

- local support groups
- congestive heart failure-specific cardiac rehab programs (which are often supported by insurance), and
- self-monitoring of weight and fluid consumption, among other resources.

CHAPTER 5

Meals That are Best for Your Heart

Your heart is a precisely honed instrument. To keep it running at its best, you must give it heart-healthy nourishment. So, you should prioritize eating a healthy diet. Certain foods are excellent for your heart, but how do you choose?

A diagnosis of heart disease has been given to more than one in 10 Americans. By selecting the right nutritional meals, the risk of cardiovascular disease, such as coronary artery disease, which can result in a heart attack or stroke, can be decreased.

The Top 25 Foods for Protecting Your Blood Vessels and Heart Are Listed Below

Discover the top nutrients that maintain a healthy heartbeat and get menu ideas for including these foods in your everyday meals.

Salmon

Salmon contains significant amounts of omega-3 fatty acids, which can reduce your risk of arrhythmias, lower triglyceride levels, slow the development of arterial plaque, and modestly lower blood pressure. The American Heart Association recommends two meals per week of omega-3-rich foods like salmon. A portion of cooked fish weighs 3.5 ounces.

Salmon is a food with several uses. For an added protein boost, add it to salads or barbecue it with a rub or marinade. Also, you may cut it up and mix it with fat-free marinara sauce in a spaghetti dish.

Salmon: Wild vs. Farmed

Does your salmon's omega-3 content depend on how it was raised? Now, many supermarkets sell salmon that has been produced on farms and that has been captured in the wild. It turns out that salmon raised on farms typically has more total fat and omega-3 fat in it. Although farmed salmon includes more saturated fat than flank steak does, the amount is still about half as high.

Flaxseed (ground)

Ground flaxseed also provides omega-3s, along with both soluble and insoluble fiber. It has one of the largest quantities of lignans, which act as both plant estrogens and antioxidants.

It's simple to incorporate ground flaxseed into your diet and you can add it to practically anything you regularly consume. It can be included in smoothies, muffin toppings, breakfast cereal, low-fat yogurt, and muffin batter.

Flaxseed oil: What Is It?

Flaxseed oil is a rich source of omega-3s, however, they are mostly of the less effective ALA type (alpha-linolenic acid). To convert ALA into omega-3, specific enzymes are required, and your body only contains a little quantity of these enzymes. This means that at most 15% of the omega-3s in flaxseed oil will be transformed into their most beneficial forms. Hence, even if you undoubtedly receive some benefit, it can be less than what the supplement label indicates.

Oatmeal

Oatmeal is a delectable breakfast option and a good source of omega-3 fatty acids. It is also a fiber powerhouse with 4 grams per cup. It also contains magnesium, potassium, and iron, among other minerals.

Oatmeal becomes an even more heart-healthy breakfast option when some fresh berries are added on top. Make whole rolled oats into oat bread, fat-free oatmeal cookies, or a turkey burger meatloaf.

Black or Kidney Beans

It uses the well-known schoolyard chant, "Beans, beans, excellent for your heart." Turns out it's true!

Soluble fiber, omega-3 fatty acids, B-complex vitamins, niacin, folate, magnesium, and calcium are all abundant in beans.

Beans have a lot of uses. They can be included in soups, stews, and salads. Or you could cook dinner with them.

Try putting black beans, corn, and onions in bell peppers or topping a whole-grain pita tostada with them. A salad with canned kidney beans, cucumber, fresh corn, onions, and peppers is topped with olive oil and apple cider vinegar. A tasty, nutritious vegetarian chili can also be made by combining black beans and kidney beans.

Almonds

It has been demonstrated that nuts reduce blood cholesterol. Almonds are a great option for a nut that is heart-healthy. These include heart-healthy monounsaturated and polyunsaturated fats, vitamin E, magnesium, calcium, fiber, and plant omega-3 fatty acids.

Almonds are quite easy to eat; you may add them to salads, yogurt, or as a trail mix snack. They can also be utilized in cooking. They can be spread over fish for a delicious crunch or added to a bowl of rice or quinoa. Without salt, almonds provide further cardiac protection.

All you need to do is watch your portion sizes and make sure your almonds are raw or dry roasted (as opposed to oil roasted). They have a lot of fat, including some saturated fat, despite being heart-healthy. Like other nuts, almonds are high in calories, so a little bit goes a long way. It's preferable to eat them in moderation.

Walnuts

The health advantages of almonds and other tree nuts are comparable to those of walnuts.

They contain plant omega-3 fatty acids, phytosterols, heart-healthy monosaturated and polyunsaturated fats, vitamin E, magnesium, folate, and fiber.

Walnuts offer salads a robust crunch to almonds. For breakfast, they pair well with muffins and pancakes.

While being heart-healthy, they contain a lot of fat and calories and should only be consumed in moderation. Like with another nut, walnut portion sizes should be considered. One serving of walnuts, which has about 200 calories, should easily fit in your palm.

Red Wine

Along with the anti-oxidant resveratrol, catechins are a group of flavonoids that are present in red wine. Flavonoids may help avoid blood clots and support the health of your blood vessels Resveratrol has been shown in the laboratory to have heart-healthy effects.

Have some wine with dinner or create a wine spritzer by combining wine and sparkling water to reduce calories while retaining many of the advantages.

However, keep in mind that the American Heart Association does not recommend that people begin drinking to solely prevent heart disease. Drinking alcohol increases your chance of becoming an alcoholic and your risk of obesity, hypertension, stroke, breast cancer, suicide, and car accidents. Drink red wine sparingly (for example, one wine glass full with a meal).

Tuna

fatty acids omega-3 that can be found in tuna. Although not as high as that of salmon, tuna nevertheless has a respectable amount of omega-3s. One serving of tuna also contains about half of your daily recommended intake of niacin, a vitamin that may improve the chances of survival for people who have suffered a heart attack.

Tuna salad with minimal mayo is an easy and satisfying noon snack. Tuna can be grilled to make a delicious supper or a wonderful addition to a salad.

Choosing Tuna Cans

Tuna in cans is one of the most popular varieties of seafood in America. Nonetheless, choosing the best can be difficult given the abundance of possibilities. The two most widely consumed types are light tuna, which is created from lesser kinds of tuna, and white tuna, which is prepared from albacore (usually skipjack). Although white has more omega-3s, it also has greater mercury levels, which are particularly harmful to expecting moms.

While some tuna is sold in water, some tuna is offered for sale in oil. In water-based tuna, omega-3 fat is far more prevalent. This is because a sizeable portion of that omega-3 fat is lost when you drain the oil from the container.

Tofu

Tofu is an excellent source of protein. Veggie cuisine. Also, it contains a lot of heart-healthy nutrients, including calcium, magnesium, potassium, niacin, and folate.

Tofu is occasionally called "bean curd" because it is made from pressed soybean curd. It is easy to make and pairs beautifully with almost any meal.

Firm tofu needs to be thinly sliced and marinated for a few hours before grilling or adding to your preferred vegetable stir-fry. For more protein, substitute tofu for the meat in pasta dishes and add slices or cubes to salads. With whole-grain bread, you can also build a sandwich with tofu, lettuce, and tomato.

Avoid Using Processed Tofu Products.

Tofu has been shown to have heart-protective effects in multiple studies, albeit it depends on how you prepare it. Tofu is not always surrounded by friends, even though it can be nourishing. Several ultra-processed foods, which have been connected to obesity and cardiovascular disease, include it. When tofu products are used in processed foods with high calories, the FDA removed some of its benefits for heart health in 2017.

Brown Rice

In addition to being delicious, brown rice is a heart-healthy eating option. Brown rice contains B-complex vitamins, magnesium, and fiber.

Almost any cuisine will taste great when brown rice is included. A straightforward and speedy lunch option is microwave-heated brown rice. Use it in stir-fries, and soups, pair it with tofu or black beans or serve it cold in an avocado salad.

Soy Milk

Soy milk is particularly nutrient-dense and contains isoflavones, a type of flavonoid. In addition to other nutrients, there are phytoestrogens, calcium, magnesium, potassium, folate, and B-complex vitamins. The protein in soy milk, as opposed to the protein found in animal milk, can help lower blood cholesterol levels and may also have other beneficial effects on the cardiovascular system.

Any dish, including your morning whole grain cereal or a smoothie, can be made using soy milk in place of dairy milk.

Blueberries

Berries are good for your heart in particular as well as the rest of your body. Blueberries are rich in fiber, the vitamins C and folate, calcium, magnesium, potassium, the antioxidants beta-carotene and lutein, the flavonoid anthocyanin, the polyphenol ellagic acid, the flavonoid anthocyanin, and many other nutrients.

Berries are an easy and convenient healthy snack to enjoy on their own, as a topping for cereal or pancakes, in a smoothie, as a garnish for low-fat yogurt, or in a salad.

Carrots

Carrots' carotenoid content is probably what most people know about them. Together with the well-known vitamin beta-carotene, carrots also contain alpha and gamma carotenes (carotenoids). A lower risk of heart disease and stroke has been associated with higher beta-carotene levels in studies.

Baby carrots are a delectable snack. They add crispness to chopped salads. Also, you can use shredded carrots in several meals, including spaghetti, muffins, and tomato sauce.

Spinach

Spinach is a powerhouse of heart-healthy nutrients, containing beta-carotene, vitamins C and E, potassium, folate, calcium, and fiber.

Spinach makes an excellent salad dressing and sandwich stuffing substitute for lettuce. Moreover, you could sneak some into pizza, fruit smoothies, and egg white omelets. Instead, you could incorporate it into your pasta preparation for an added health benefit.

Fresh or frozen spinach?

The response is contingent upon how long it has been sitting. Fresh spinach contains more folate than frozen spinach, and some studies suggest that folate may lower your risk of developing heart disease. There is a drawback though: fresh spinach loses its folate over time. Hence, whether your fresh spinach has been kept for a week in the refrigerator or has traveled a long way to get to your table, frozen spinach might be healthier.

Broccoli

The powerful nutrients in broccoli include beta-carotene, vitamins C and E, potassium, folate, calcium, and fiber.

Brown rice meals, salads, vegetable dips, and soups with broccoli are all wonderful. A certain way to improve the health of your heart is to increase your diet of broccoli.

Sweet Potato

Sweet potatoes are a fantastic nutrient source. Sweet potatoes are a special low-fat source of vitamin E in addition to carrying vitamins A and C. They also contain fiber, potassium, folate, calcium, and calcium. When you eat their skins, you also get an additional dose of fiber.

Practically any preparation method for a sweet potato will produce a tasty result. Completely bake it and then top it with vegetables. Cut it into wedges, then bake them in the oven until crisp. Sweet potatoes can be processed in a food processor to create a silky soup. As a side dish, they taste great when mashed.

Sweet potatoes are not the same as yams. Yams are also a good source of nutrition, but sweet potatoes have more fiber, vitamins, and minerals.

Red Bell Peppers

Acidic, crunchy red bell peppers are rich in beta-carotene and lutein, two heart-healthy minerals, fiber, B-complex vitamins, folate, and potassium (carotenoids).

Peppers are delicious in salads and sandwiches, or you can slice them up and consume them as a snack while still fresh. Roast or grill them to make a hearty side dish that will enhance sauces or main meals.

Regarding the heart-healthy chemicals in bell peppers, color is important. Red peppers, for instance, have high levels of beta-carotene. Even while yellow bells are healthy in many other ways, they hardly contain any beta-carotene at all.

Asparagus

Beta-carotene, lutein, folate, fiber, and vitamins B and C are all present in asparagus, making it a nutrient-rich vegetable.

Asparagus makes a great side dish that is heart-healthy. After lightly grilling or steaming the meal, cover it with some balsamic vinaigrette. To increase the nutritional content of salads, stews, or casseroles, add.

Oranges

The optimum snack is an orange. They also include fiber, potassium, vitamin C, alpha- and beta-carotene, lutein, flavones (flavonoids), potassium, folate, and the antioxidant beta-cryptoxanthin. Also, they are juicy and loaded with vital nutrients.

Because it tastes best that way, the fruit should be consumed whole. You may add orange slices to salads, yogurt, and even chicken meals. It is still advised to eat the fruit whole even though orange juice might offer some of the same benefits.

Tomatoes

The variety of nutrients in tomatoes, including beta- and alpha-carotene, lycopene, lutein (carotenoids), vitamin C, potassium, folate, and fiber, make them heart-healthy food. Research on lycopene as a possible preventative measure for cardiovascular disease is still unclear.

You can add raw tomatoes to salads or sandwiches. When cooked, they are the perfect ingredient in pasta recipes and make excellent sauces.

Acorn Squash

Acorn squash, another heart-healthy food, also has beta-carotene and lutein (carotenoids), the B complex and C vitamins, folate, calcium, magnesium, potassium, and fiber.

A delicious winter dish is baked acorn squash. Before roasting, split the squash in half, scoop out the seeds, and fill it with brown rice and vegetables.

Cantaloupe

Cantaloupe is a summertime classic that also contains numerous heart-healthy nutrients, including alpha-, beta-, and lutein (carotenoids), B-complex and C vitamins, folate, potassium, and fiber.

Simply slice up some cantaloupe and enjoy it whenever you want! Make a fresh fruit salad out of some of them or combine some of them into a smoothie.

Papaya

Papaya contains the carotenoids lutein, beta-cryptoxanthin, and beta-carotene. Vitamins A and C are also a part of your diet, along with folate, calcium, and potassium.

Papaya goes nicely with salmon, a heart-healthy dish. A fruit salad, smoothie, popsicle, salsa, or even on the grill can benefit from its inclusion.

Dark Chocolate

glad tidings Both the heart-healthy antioxidant resveratrol and the blood pressure-lowering cocoa phenols can be found in chocolate.

To get the advantages, stick to dark chocolate with a 70% cocoa content or above, and remember that since chocolate is high in calories, fat, and sugar, moderation is key. There is just a need for one serving.

Tea

Tea has flavonoids and catechins, which are similar to those in red wine and may help prevent blood clots from forming and maintain the health of your blood vessels. For its anti-inflammatory properties, green tea has received special appreciation.

A thorough study involving more than 6,000 adults found that drinking tea may reduce your risk of getting cardiac issues. According to the study, those who drank 1-3 cups of tea daily had higher coronary calcium scores. Coronary calcium may indicate the onset of future cardiac problems, such as a heart attack or stroke.

Tea is welcome hot or cold. Perhaps add some lemon. If you want to extract more antioxidants from the tea, use hotter water and let it steep for three to five minutes at the very least. Avoid using sugar and cream as they add extra calories and fat.

CHAPTER 6

Substitutions for Heart-Wise Eating

Cook Your Catch

How you prepare your fish has a big impact on your heart. Instead of frying your meal, bake or grill it to limit the quantity of artery-clogging saturated fat. Baked grouper with lemon, delicate cod, or tilapia with seasonings. Cook some snapper, sea bass, or other hard fish on the grill. In comparison to fried fish, each serving will contain about 70 fewer calories and 50 percent less saturated fat.

Choose Greek (yogurt) over Mayo

In place of all or a portion of the heavy mayo in your tuna or chicken salad, dietician and chef Katie Cavuto Boyle suggests substituting nonfat Greek yogurt. As an alternative, top a lean turkey sandwich with a dollop of this thick, tangy yogurt and a ton of vegetables. You'll substitute calcium and protein calories for those from fat.

Use Flaxseeds in Baking

You can substitute flaxseeds for eggs when making muffins, quick bread, pancakes, cookies, and even chocolate cake. A big egg can be substituted with 3 teaspoons of water, 3 tablespoons of powdered flaxseed, and 1/8 teaspoon of baking powder. You'll consume more fiber if you steer clear of egg yolk cholesterol. Both changes can help you keep your cholesterol under control.

Casserole With Reduced-Fat Cheese

Your nana's recipe probably calls for the full-fat version of ricotta because it is widely used in lasagna and other cheese bakes. By choosing low-fat, you may cut 9 grams of saturated fat from each meal. Maintaining a daily intake of fewer than 16 grams for heart health is highly advantageous. As long as the cheese is lower in fat, you can have ricotta or cottage cheese. Ground turkey breast with less fat is a heart-healthy substitute for rich ground beef.

Choose Wholesome Fruit

The fruit has a lot of fiber, few calories, and is good for your weight and blood pressure. Therefore stay away from fruit that has been canned in syrup and choose fresh stuff instead. In just one cup of peaches in "light" syrup, 33 grams of sugar are present. Serving a little candy bar next to a dish of juicy, crisp peach slices would be comparable to doing that.

Cheese, Cream? Whisk It Up!

You can still spread cream cheese on your whole-wheat bagel in the morning. Purchase the whipped variety from the dairy department. You may cut back on calories and saturated fat by almost half. Compare: 100 calories are contained in two teaspoons of one popular brand. The amount of saturated fat before lunch is 6 grams or one-third of your daily allotment! The whipped variation has 60 fewer calories and 60% less saturated fat.

Avoid Pressing That Orange

Breakfast and orange juice just seem to go together. However, if you want a citrus kick, a real orange is preferred. Almost no fiber and about 21 grams of sugar are included in one cup of orange juice. While having somewhat less sugar, a large orange has more than six times the amount of heart-healthy fiber (about 17 grams).

Turkey Sausage, please!

Shop supermarkets carefully. If you replace pig or beef sausage with low-fat turkey sausage, your heart will thank you. Simmer it with beans that are high in fiber and veggies. Only 1.5 grams of saturated fat are present in three lean turkey sausage links for breakfast. In a comparable pig sausage, unhealthy saturated fat is three times as abundant.

Unwind With Fruit

Do you consider ice cream to be the best comfort food? A half cup of delicious, frozen blueberries that have been mixed with nonfat yogurt can help you stay cool. This delicious treat has almost none of the 14 grams of saturated fat found in some pricey ice creams made with indulgent toppings. Also, you cut back on calories and sugar, which is good news if you're attempting to lose weight.

How to Prepare Oatmeal

Oatmeal has long been advocated as a strategy to lower cholesterol due to its soluble fiber. Yet, there may be 15 grams (three teaspoons!) of sugar in a packet of quick raisin and spice oats. Make oatmeal instead of using real oats. Add a few raisins and a sprinkle of cinnamon to a mixture with only around 9 grams of sugar. Although it takes longer, it can significantly affect your heart and weight.

CHAPTER 7

A 7-Day Meal Plan That Compresses Breakfast, Lunch, And Dinner with Ingredients and Preparation Instruction for Congestive Heart Failure Patient

Congestive heart failure (CHF) sufferers must maintain a balanced diet to control their condition. Limiting salt and saturated fat while consuming lots of whole grains, fruits, vegetables, and lean proteins are typical components of a heart-healthy diet. A typical meal plan for CHF patients that includes suggestions for breakfast, lunch, and dinner is provided below:

Day 1:

Breakfast: Oatmeal with berries and almonds

1/2 cup old-fashioned rolled oats

1 cup water

1/4 cup fresh or frozen berries

1 tablespoon chopped almonds

Cook oats according to the package instructions. Top with berries and almonds.

Lunch: Turkey and avocado sandwich

2 slices whole-grain bread

2 ounces sliced turkey breast

1/4 avocado, sliced

1 small tomato, sliced

1 tablespoon Dijon mustard

Layer turkey, avocado, and tomato on the bread. Spread mustard on the remaining piece of bread. To assemble the sandwich, press the slices together.

Dinner: Grilled salmon with roasted vegetables

4-ounce salmon fillet

1/2 cup mixed vegetables (such as bell peppers, zucchini, and onion)

1 tablespoon olive oil

1/4 teaspoon dried herbs (such as oregano or thyme)

Preheat the oven to 375°F. Toss vegetables with olive oil and herbs. For 20 to 25 minutes, roast until soft in the oven. Grill the salmon over medium-high heat for 3–4 minutes per side, or until cooked through.

Day 2:

Breakfast: Greek yogurt with fruit and granola

1/2 cup plain Greek yogurt

1/4 cup fresh or frozen berries

1/4 cup low-sugar granola

Mix yogurt, berries, and granola in a bowl.

Lunch: Grilled chicken salad

2 cups mixed greens

4 ounces grilled chicken breast, sliced

1/4 cup cherry tomatoes, halved

1/4 cup sliced cucumber

1 tablespoon balsamic vinaigrette

Arrange greens on a plate. Top with chicken, tomatoes, and cucumber. Drizzle with vinaigrette.

Dinner: Lentil soup

1/2 cup dried lentils

1/2 cup chopped vegetables (such as onion, carrot, and celery)

1/2 cup low-sodium chicken broth

1/2 cup water

1/2 teaspoon dried herbs (such as basil or oregano)

Rinse the lentils and drain. Combine lentils, vegetables, broth, water, and herbs in a pot. Bring to a boil, then reduce heat and simmer for 30-35 minutes, until lentils are tender.

Day 3:

Breakfast: Veggie omelet

2 eggs

1/4 cup chopped vegetables (such as bell pepper, onion, and spinach)

1 teaspoon olive oil

Whisk the eggs in a bowl. Over medium heat, warm oil in a nonstick skillet. Add the vegetables and sauté until tender. Pour eggs over vegetables and cook until set.

Lunch: Tuna salad lettuce wraps

1 can tuna, drained

1 tablespoon chopped celery

1 tablespoon chopped red onion

1 tablespoon chopped parsley

1 tablespoon Dijon mustard

1 tablespoon plain Greek yogurt

2-3 large lettuce leaves

Mix tuna, celery, onion, parsley, mustard, and yogurt in a bowl. Fill lettuce leaves with the mixture, then roll them up.

Dinner: Grilled tofu with stir-fried vegetables

4 ounces firm tofu, sliced

1/2 cup mixed vegetables (such as bell peppers, broccoli, and carrots)

1 teaspoon sesame oil

1 teaspoon low-sodium soy sauce

Grill tofu over medium-high heat for 3–4 minutes per side, until browned. Stir-fry vegetables in sesame oil and soy sauce for 3–4 minutes, until tender.

Day 4:

Breakfast: Smoothie bowl

1/2 cup frozen mixed berries

1/2 banana

1/2 cup plain Greek yogurt

1/4 cup low-sugar granola

Blend berries, bananas, and yogurt in a blender. Place the mixture in a bowl and sprinkle some granola on top.

Lunch: Turkey chili

4 ounces of ground turkey

1/2 cup canned diced tomatoes

1/2 cup washed and drained canned kidney beans

1/2 cup low-sodium chicken broth

1/4 teaspoon chili powder

Brown the turkey in a pot over medium heat. Add tomatoes, beans, broth, and chili powder. Simmer for 20 to 25 minutes to melt the flavors.

Dinner: Baked cod with quinoa and green beans

4-ounce cod fillet

1/2 cup cooked quinoa

1/2 cup green beans, steamed

1 teaspoon olive oil

1/four teaspoon of dry herbs (such as rosemary or thyme)

Preheat the oven to 375°F. Rub cod with olive oil and herbs. Bake for 12–15 minutes, until cooked through. Serve with quinoa and green beans.

Day 5:

Breakfast: Banana and nut butter on whole-grain bread

2 slices whole-grain bread

1/4 cup nut butter (such as almond or peanut butter)

1/2 banana, sliced

Toast bread. Spread nut butter on each slice. Top with banana slices.

Lunch: Grilled chicken and vegetable skewers

4 ounces grilled chicken breast, cubed

1/2 cup mixed vegetables (such as cherry tomatoes, bell peppers, and zucchini)

1 teaspoon olive oil

Thread chicken and vegetables onto skewers. Brush with olive oil. Grill for 3 to 4 minutes on each side, or until well cooked, over medium-high heat.

Dinner: will be spaghetti squash with meatballs made of turkey.

1/2 medium spaghetti squash

1/2 cup canned marinara sauce

2 ounces of ground turkey

1/4 teaspoon dried herbs (such as basil or oregano)

Preheat the oven to 375°F. By splitting the spaghetti squash in half, the seeds can be removed. 30 to 40 minutes are needed to roast something tender in the oven. Over medium heat, brown the turkey in the pan. Add marinara sauce and herbs. Simmer the meatballs for a further 10 to 15 minutes, or until done. Serve meatballs over spaghetti squash.

Day 6:

Breakfast: Greek yogurt with nuts and honey

1/2 cup plain Greek yogurt

1 tablespoon chopped nuts (such as walnuts or almonds)

1 teaspoon honey

Mix yogurt, nuts, and honey in a bowl.

Lunch: Grilled vegetable sandwich

2 slices whole-grain bread

1/4 cup sliced grilled vegetables (such as eggplant, zucchini, and bell peppers)

1 tablespoon hummus

Toast bread. Spread hummus on one slice. Layer vegetables on the other slice. Press slices

together.

Dinner: Baked salmon with roasted asparagus

4-ounce salmon fillet

1/2 bunch of asparagus, trimmed

1 teaspoon olive oil

1/4 teaspoon dried herbs (such as dill or parsley)

Preheat oven to 375°F. Rub salmon with olive oil and herbs. Bake for 12-15 minutes, until cooked through. Toss asparagus with olive oil and roast in the oven for 10-12 minutes, until tender.

Day 7:

Breakfast: Avocado toast with tomato

2 slices whole-grain bread

1/2 avocado, mashed

1/2 tomato, sliced

Toast bread. Spread mashed avocado on each slice. Top with tomato slices.

Lunch: Chicken and vegetable stir-fry

4 ounces grilled chicken breast, sliced

1/2 cup mixed vegetables (such as broccoli, carrots, and snow peas)

1 teaspoon sesame oil

1 teaspoon low-sodium soy sauce

Stir-fry chicken and vegetables in sesame oil and soy sauce for 3-4 minutes, until heated through.

Dinner: Lentil soup with whole-grain bread

1/2 cup cooked lentils

1/2 cup low-sodium chicken broth

1/4 cup chopped vegetables (such as onion, carrot, and celery)

1/4 teaspoon of dried herbs (such as thyme or basil)

Combine lentils, broth, vegetables, and herbs in a pot. To combine the flavors, simmer for 20 to 25 minutes. Serve with whole-grain bread.

Note: This meal plan is intended as a general guide for individuals with congestive heart failure. It is important to consult with a healthcare provider or registered dietitian to personalize a meal plan based on individual needs and medical conditions.

CONCLUSION

Congestive heart failure (CHF) is a serious condition that could be fatal and that needs to be properly managed with a mix of medicines, lifestyle changes, and regular medical care. Although CHF can have a large negative influence on a person's quality of life, numerous things can be done to enhance results and lessen symptoms. People with CHF can improve their health and well-being by eating a heart-healthy diet, working closely with healthcare professionals, and exercising frequently. People should be aware of the dangers and indicators of CHF and seek medical help right away if they see any warning signs. Many people with CHF can enjoy happy, active lives with the right care and management.

Here is a heartfelt poem I wrote to let you know you are not alone.

You have the power to start with every heartbeat.

One more day, one more opportunity to live your life and dance.

Although CHF may make you feel heavy

You can still grin instead of pout.

Every moment is filled with joy.

Don't ignore each day; instead, embrace it.

Deepen your breath and experience the air.

Know you are here in your lungs.

Who you do not depend on your sickness.

You're a powerful, resolute individual.

True, things might be a little different now.

Nonetheless, that does not lessen its significance.

It appears that you can still pursue your aspirations and fully enjoy life.

So don't give up and hold onto hope.

You are capable; you have the power.

Be certain that you are sufficient as you move forward.

You have a strong heart and soul and are a warrior.

Just remember that there are caring people around you during those difficult times.

You have a community, so you are not alone.

Who will be there in unison with you?

So, maintain your grip and never let go.

With every heartbeat, you have the opportunity to live your life filled with love and romance. The world needs you. You are not alone.

Printed in Great Britain
by Amazon

25075301R00059